USBORNE

Expert advice from
Abbee McLatchie

**Deputy CEO,
National Youth Agency**

USBORNE

Written by
Holly Bathie & Alex Frith

Designed by
Stephanie Jeffries

Illustrated by
Jack Brougham & Laura Wood

Edited by
Felicity Brooks

Glossary words

Look out for (**key words**) picked out throughout this book. Each one is explained in the Glossary at the end of the book on pages 168–171.

Introduction

This book is about...

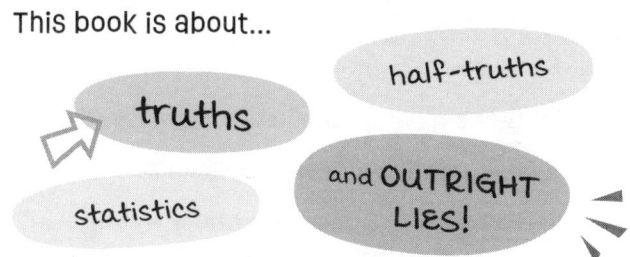

truths

half-truths

statistics

and OUTRIGHT LIES!

It will show you the techniques people use to get you to **buy stuff**, or **vote for them**, or to **turn you against somebody**. It'll even show you how there are times when someone tells you a lie – that you *know* is a lie – and it can STILL make you doubt the truth.

What actually is FAKE NEWS?

Fake news is when somebody presents information about what's going on in the world (the news), but that information is either a **deliberate lie** – known as disinformation, or **accidentally wrong** – known as misinformation.

Here's a piece of good news: *truth DOES exist*. In fact, MOST of the news that you read or see or hear about is reliable. That's if it comes from **mainstream news outlets**, for example, the BBC, Al Jazeera, or some other major national news source. This kind of news reporting is known as **journalism**.

Mainstream news outlets need to verify their stories. They don't always get it right, but this book will explain WHY.

This book will also give you the opportunity to practise making up some fake news of your own. The fact is, if you learn

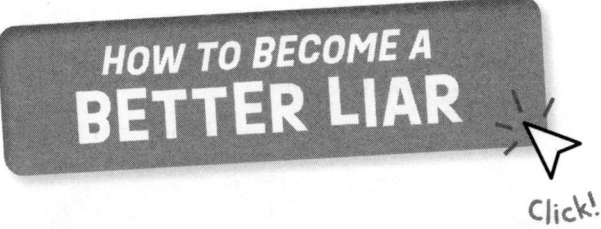

Click!

and discover HOW successful lies are created, you will become much better at **spotting fake news** out in the world.

FUN FACT:

The phrase "fake news" was only made popular in the 2010s. But the idea of telling news that isn't true is as old as communication itself.

Often, when someone cries,

"fake news!"

it's less about them identifying a story as FALSE and more about them saying:

I don't like what I'm hearing. And if you agree with me, then we're on the same side and can be friends!

If you've ever fallen for a piece of fake news,

it's NOT YOUR FAULT.

This book will help you see why that happens, and give you lots of great tips so it will be less likely to happen to you in future.

ANYBODY can make mistakes and fall for other people's tricks, **NO MATTER HOW CLEVER THEY ARE.**

Contents

Chapter 1
The fake content business — 13

Challenge 1:
Think like a MISINFORMER — 38

Quiz: **Can you spot fake news?** — 40

Chapter 2
Falling for fake news — 41

Challenge 2:
Think like a SCHEMER — 64

Quiz: **Let's test your brain...** — 66

Chapter 3
Reaching a wide audience — 67

Challenge 3:
Think like an INFLUENCER — 82

Chapter 4

What's the angle?   85

Challenge 4:
Think like a CONSPIRACY THEORIST   112

Chapter 5

Facts v figures   115

Challenge 5:
Think like a POLITICIAN   142

Quiz: **Taking a closer look**   144

Chapter 6

Staying ahead of scammers   145

Quiz: **How scam-savvy are you?**   162

Glossary   168

Index   172

References   174

Meet successful (influencer) Max Green. You'll follow his exploits throughout this book.

The Pigeon Today

SOCIAL MEDIA STAR IN TROUBLE

Popular online personality Max Green, AKA **maX.GameController**, has had his knuckles rapped by the Advertising Standards Authority (ASA) over undeclared PAID product promotions. Green claimed it was a "genuine mistake" not labelling six recent videos with 'AD', even though he was being paid to produce them by brands such as **TOP BRAND SPORTSWEAR**, and global soft drinks giant **FLOAT-YOUR-BOAT**.

Green's channel is popular with younger viewers. His videos often feature him in a tracksuit, swigging from a drinks bottle, as he sweats up a virtual mountain or fights off crocodiles.

Max Green, pictured here, promised to "do better next time", while the ASA has vowed to crack down on influencers who flout the rules by using hidden advertising that misleads their fans.

Max Green is made up, but this news story is based on TRUE stories about REAL influencers.

Chapter 1

The fake content business

At some point, many of us will have had our heads turned by a **FAKE NEWS** story.

~ You KNOW it ~
MAX GREEN WAS SET UP!

*Super influencer and nice guy, Max Green, is the latest target of **The Pigeon Today**'s campaign against successful people.*

A little birdie who works at 'The Pigeon' tells me they called the ASA about Max's small mistake with his videos, so THEY could get the first scoop.

And that's NOT THE ONLY NEWS SITE PEDDLING RUBBISH. Heard the one about the sky being blue?

CLICK HERE FOR THE TRUTH

We may have even clicked on it, read it, shared it or talked to others about it. That's why we ALL have a part to play in either the _spread of_, or the _prevention of_, fake news.

FAKE NEWS TYPE 1: Misinformation

Misinformation is information that... ISN'T. Misinformation is *inaccurate* or *out-of-date information* that is mistakenly presented – or interpreted – as fact. It might take the form of just one sentence. For example:

A vague news headline — **SUNLIGHT BAD FOR YOU***

An out-of-context statistic — **20% LESS HARMFUL****

A recirculated old meme — **'GANGNAM STYLE' REACTION VIDEOS VOTED FUNNIEST THING EVER*****

All it takes is just one person *misunderstanding* that information and *forwarding it on*... for confusion to spread.

*If you don't wear sunscreen.
**Than what?
***According to a poll from 2012.

Making mistakes

Misinformation lacks accuracy. If you come across a figure or statistic* in an article, there should be some small print you can check that tells you where the evidence for it came from.

> You should also be able to see:
> - the DATE the article was written.
> - the NAME of the news outlet.
> - the AUTHOR'S NAME (the **byline**).
>
> If there's a photo:
> - the NAME OF THE PHOTOGRAPHER should also be credited.

If some of this information is *missing* or *wrong*, there's always a chance that a simple mistake has crept in.

However...

If an article contains **NONE** of these, then it's likely you can just *ignore it entirely*.

*You can read more about statistics in Chapter 5.

> **WHOOPS!**

Reliable news outlets will publish **corrections** to their articles <u>as soon as they are aware of an error</u>. Corrections are published in the original place the mistake is made, e.g. if the mistake is in a *newspaper article*, the correction will be published in the *newspaper*.

> There's no way we can erase THIS!

BUT when a mistake is shared on *social media*, it can be hard for any corrections to find their way to the same audience.

TRUST THE SCIENCE?

Technical-sounding **scientific information** *often feels trustworthy. But errors can still creep into science journalism. Any news you're interested in sharing is worth a second read through to make sure it's accurate.*

The evidence is... missing

Science can move forward at a slow pace, and the kind of **major breakthrough** in health or technology that sells newspapers doesn't come along too often. So, sometimes a news site can jump on any sniff of a 'story' and get it out there <u>before the evidence is in</u>.

Once the story is published, *the evidence may be forgotten*. Which can make the popular headline: **RESEARCH HAS SHOWN...** a nonsense phrase.

Now where did I put that research?

Well I haven't seen it.

The (mainstream media) can often be under pressure to

PUBLISH, PUBLISH, PUBLISH,

resulting in some vague science articles which are more likely to CONFUSE than INFORM, leading to the spread of misinformation.

So...

...even for stories published in the mainstream media, you should

DO YOUR OWN RESEARCH.

Something that catches your eye and seems surprising, outrageous, exciting or tugs at your heartstrings might be missing **information** and **accuracy**.

Start by checking the story on specific science news sites. They MIGHT include references to named scientific studies. It can be a bit of extra work, but it should fill in any missing information. Most importantly, it prevents sharing accidental MISINFORMATION.

FAKE NEWS TYPE 2: Disinformation

Disinformation is *deliberately untrue content* which is created and shared in order to convince people to *think a certain way*.

> As it's FAKE NEWS, it purposefully doesn't contain evidence for the reader to examine and **verify** elsewhere.

Disinformation around

- vaccines
- food supplements
- weight loss

is especially common online. Our health is important to us, so fake 'health news' headlines are good choices for (**clickbait**) articles and **scams**.

Doctors don't want you to know about this ONE SIMPLE TRICK...

SHARE

Secret 'truths'

One famous kind of disinformation goes by the name **conspiracy theory**. There's a clue in the name:

THEORY

These are STORIES based on *creative ideas*, and NOT on *factual information*. Conspiracy theorists claim that groups of powerful people, especially experts, keep secrets and hide evidence.

Conspiracy theories around health can gain support because people may feel at the mercy of medical professionals who have more information than them.

> Our gut simply cannot absorb medicine in pill form.*

> No way! Pharmacists have been LYING to us for decades!

*Totally untrue, in case you were wondering.

Lack of information and *feeling powerless* can drive people to seek out 'alternative' theories, medicines and professionals... who might just be ANYTHING BUT.

Dr. Quack
Medical Expert
in Guesswork and Speculation

MEDICAL MYTHS

A very well-known piece of disinformation is the claim that:

> "The MMR* vaccine causes autism."

This claim is <u>old</u>. It was made by then-doctor Andrew Wakefield in 1998, and was exposed as FRAUDULENT by 2010. Yet, it still pops up online today.

Wakefield's article was published in *The Lancet*, a respected medical journal. Journals are supposed to be checked and verified for accuracy before they are published. Being published in *The Lancet* meant lots of people took the story at face value.

*Measles, Mumps and Rubella

AND YET...

Lots of doctors and other experts questioned the study as soon as the paper was published. In 2010 the journal finally **retracted** the article (which is the equivalent of 'unpublishing' it) for a number of reasons, including:

1. The number of children sampled in the **study was too small** to provide a statistically significant result. (There's more about statistics and studies in Chapter 5.)

2. Wakefield had not disclosed the fact that the children included in the study were `cherry-picked`.

3. Wakefield had not revealed that he had conducted the study on behalf of lawyers who **had an `agenda`** and that he stood to earn money from his 'findings'. (There's more on hidden agendas in Chapter 4.)

THE VERDICT IS IN

As medical studies go, this one was <u>useless</u>, and Andrew Wakefield's false claim led to him being told he could no longer legally work as a doctor. There have been multiple *properly-conducted studies* carried out since 1998 into a link between any vaccine and autism, and NO LINK has been found. People still want to know what causes autism, though, so until that is discovered, this false claim will probably still get shared around.

> It only takes one person casting doubt on something for other people to start doubting as well. It's human nature.

That lady who's on trial... do you think she did it?

She's ON TRIAL — she must be guilty of something...

FAKE NEWS TYPE 3: Propaganda

(Propaganda) is the king of fake news: organized, slick and targeted. Propaganda is a *careful campaign of disinformation*, usually about world events or politics. It's used by wealthy people, organizations and governments who have a lot to gain (such as more money and more power), by successfully **influencing public opinion**. Sometimes this *unites society* against an enemy. Other times it *creates divisions* in society to weaken it.

An unstable and divided society is more vulnerable to attempts by individuals and organizations to impose their own form of control.

COMMON TRICKS EMPLOYED BY PROPAGANDISTS...

Online propaganda can be *very subtle*. It can start with some carefully-placed comments on forums, or social media posts, playing on people's **emotions** to get the disinformation ball rolling.

People who feel:

ANGRY   *offended*   SCARED   excited

will share content without considering who came up with it, or what its **agenda** might be.

HiddenTruthSniffer
I KNEW IT! I've ALWAYS said that.

MinotaurQue5ta
UNBELIEVABLE!!!
Everyone needs to see this.

Propagandists love (**trolling**) people, to push them into rival groups. They use (**polarizing**) language to set those groups further apart. This can set off a 'snowball effect' of *misunderstanding*, *judgements*, *outrage* and even *violence* of one group against another.

Propagandists can also impersonate genuine news sites, or create fake academics to spread disinformation. **Their deviousness knows no limits!**

Creating a smokescreen

Sometimes a propagandist's task is to *deflect attention* away from any goings-on that they don't want scrutinized by the media and the public. This is known as creating a smokescreen, to *hide information* and *confuse people* into stumbling in another direction. Creating a smokescreen can involve casting doubt upon the origin of facts. For example, attacking the motives or the credentials of an expert. Smokescreens can also involve promoting conspiracy theories in several places online, to imply that a large number of people don't buy into the mainstream news. This trick undermines the public's trust in facts and experts. It was deliberately used by climate-change deniers in the 1990s, and it's still going on today.

Blending in

The most effective propaganda makes sure to look as CONVINCING as possible. It encourages emotional responses, but mimics mainstream news reporting by including just enough actual facts to make their narrative appear as believable as the truth.

> **The aim is to promote DOUBT.**

With doubt comes LACK OF TRUST, and a desire to *look elsewhere* for something that appears reliable.

AI and fake news

Propagandists use **artificial intelligence (AI)** to create sophisticated fake news, such as (deepfakes). These are images, videos or audio of well-known people that have been carefully edited to make them *appear to say or do things they never said or did*. Deepfakes are made either to **discredit** a person or to **imply support** for the creator's cause.

A video or image might be a deepfake if:

- The person's FEATURES, or the BACKGROUND, look blurry or inaccurate.

- In a video, the EMOTION on their face or their GESTURES don't seem to match what they are saying.

CLIMATE CHANGE IS A MYTH.

- In a video or audio clip, the WAY THEY SPEAK is inconsistent.

- What they are doing or saying is OUT OF CHARACTER.

I think we convinced them.

But the truth is, deepfakes can be VERY convincing. If you aren't sure, check. It's part of the job of mainstream news sites to verify – or debunk – potential deepfakes. If a popular video clip isn't mentioned at all by mainstream media, it's probably FAKE.

>> WATCH OUT FOR BOTS!

Propagandists also make great use of **bots**, which are computer programs designed to run a repetitive task, such as *reposting disinformation over and over again*.

AI chatbots can be used in large numbers by propagandists to go on forums and pretend to be real people, influencing conversations and steering them in a particular direction.

How to spot a social media bot:

- The account posts a lot all day and night — BOTS NEVER GET TIRED.

- The account is REPETITIVE and talks about the same thing over and over.

Bots can be hidden behind fake accounts, using stolen or fake photos, and even have fake followers. Fiendish!

> Why is there so much fake news out there?

You can't just say anything you like on social media – there are (defamation) laws about what you can and can't say about people, even online. However, there is no specific 'fake news' police force. News changes daily, so social media platforms can't keep on top of all the hundreds of articles and bits of gossip circulating online every day.

Misinformation can be accidentally created by anyone – from confused presidents, to the person who sits next to you on the bus.

Disinformation can be created by any person or group with a particular agenda. People get away with posting under false names in the online world, and **it's difficult to know who is REALLY behind any online account**. The truth is, ANYONE can make fake news.

Ah, but does a bit of fake news REALLY matter?

Spoof news stories, or satire, circulate online all the time. You might think you can recognize these, especially if they pop up on April Fool's Day, and that you wouldn't fall for them. YOU wouldn't share something misleading... would you? No one wants to get fooled into believing something that isn't true. At best, that's embarrassing. BUT, at worst, falling for – and spreading – fake news could cost you your REPUTATION, your HEALTH or your MONEY. *Or someone else's.*

Think like a MISINFORMER

Imagine YOU wanted to create a fun made-up story to fool your mates. How would you convince them? (Whoops, it spread online!)

DID YOU KNOW...?
When the first Disneyland opened, one of the original characters you could meet was BUGS BUNNY.

Grab attention

Start with an interesting-sounding story that would be **AMAZING if it were true.**

> How cool would it be if you could still meet Bugs Bunny at Disneyland.

Get stooges to help

A **stooge** is a person who is in on the joke with you. Find some stooges and get them each to share their story online of when **THEY met Bugs Bunny at Disneyland.**

It doesn't have to be a TRUE story, remember.

Use deepfakes

> Pics or it didn't happen...

Why not **use AI to generate some photos** showing Bugs Bunny among a crowd of Disney characters? It's hard to tell the difference between a real photo and an AI image.

The REAL story behind the lie...

The idea that a Bugs Bunny character was ever walking around Disneyland is NOT TRUE – it was part of an experiment run by psychologist Elizabeth Loftus.

Loftus tested a large group of volunteers who had all been to the original Disneyland as kids in the 1950s and 1960s. She gave them a fake pamphlet advertising the theme park that looked like it was made in the 1950s. Some of the photos inside showed Bugs Bunny.

When Loftus asked her volunteers if any of them had seen Bugs Bunny when they went to Disneyland, 30% of them said "YES". They were convinced they could remember seeing him, or even meeting him, and came up with different stories to explain how this was possible.

But Bugs Bunny isn't a Disney character! It NEVER happened.

Can you spot fake news?

It's not always easy. All of these stories *really were* reported as news, but which were TRUE?

THE WHOLE COUNTRY OF AUSTRALIA IS MOVING NORTH! ADJUST YOUR SATNAV

DEAD GORILLA WINS 11,000 VOTES IN PRESIDENTIAL ELECTION!

NEWS CHANNEL SUES GOVERNMENT FOR THE RIGHT TO TELL LIES

Answers:

1. TRUE! Very gradually, Australia IS moving north, and this does affect old satnav systems.
2. FAKE! This story was reported by some non-mainstream news sites in 2016, but it's totally bogus.
3. FAKE! One US news channel accused another of doing this, but it's totally untrue.

How can you tell REAL from FAKE?

Sometimes you just CAN'T. But you can check if it's being reported by multiple mainstream news outlets. If so, it's more likely to be true.

Chapter

2

Falling for fake news

YOU wouldn't fall for a fake news story...

...would you?

You *certainly* wouldn't believe in a conspiracy theory – you're far too intelligent for that!

Did you repost that YouKNOWit story? You know that's fake news, right?

What? No way! It's pretty convincing.

Well actually, it's all too easy to believe a piece of fake news. In the right situation, *almost anyone* can end up being taken in by some misinformation, disinformation or propaganda.

The important thing to remember is that it's NOT YOUR FAULT. Here's a pair of *scary statistics* to show how much of a problem fake-news-sharing really is:

- A 2018 study* of Twitter (now called X), checking data from 2006–2017, showed that most samples of TRUE NEWS struggled to reach just 1,000 people.

- Meanwhile, samples of FALSE NEWS from the same time period spread to 1,000 people as a *minimum* — and often reached as many as 100,000 people.

*You can find references for this and other studies on page 174.

It's human nature

Falling for fake news *can* and *does* happen to people all the time, and a big reason for this is to do with **human psychology**.

> Psychology is all about how people think and behave, and about how brains work.

One way to understand why fake news is such a **BIG** problem – why so many of us fall for it, and especially why we love *sharing* it – is to look at a few key points psychologists have discovered...

Humans are social creatures

> Human beings, in general, like to live in groups. We've evolved that way.

Most people live in a small family group, but can also be part of large family groups, and spend a lot of time in *even bigger groups,* such as at school or in a job.

> Pretty much everything about our brains is designed so that they work best around other people.

One of the consequences of being social animals is that our brains tell us to surround ourselves with friends – *in real life and in our online lives.*

Our brains are *designed* to trust the people closest to us.

Humans LOVE sharing information

Like lots of animals that live in groups, humans have developed a clever survival strategy: telling each other where to go to *find food*, and where not to go to *avoid danger*.

Some animals have developed a further strategy: LYING. For many creatures, that could be as simple as hiding a stash of food just for themselves. But humans take the strategy of lying to a whole new level...

Information spreads from one person to another within a small group very quickly.

Humans use the internet as a tool to share *everything they've ever learned*: knowledge, skills and stories. Many stories, often the least reliable ones, are about other people – **GOSSIP**.

Reputation matters

There are two reasons people spread gossip. Both are about **reputation**.

Reason 1: to boost OUR OWN reputation (or 'rep'). People *love* being the first to find out something new. That's why our brains push us to share new information quickly, even if it's *secret* information that we probably shouldn't.

It's a kind of boasting, and it makes us look **important.**

Gossiping is a way to build up a rep for yourself as someone who is 'in the know', who other people want to keep in touch with so that *they* can stay on top of gossip.

Reason 2: to affect SOMEONE ELSE'S reputation. Gossip is nearly always a story about another person. Sometimes it's a nice story, but more often it isn't. Whether or not the story is *true* rarely seems to matter.

Did they do something amazing, like save a person's life?

This makes their rep go up.

Did they do something awful, like cheat on their partner?

This can make their rep go way, way down.

Nearly true or REALLY true?

Of course, it's ideal if the gossip that *you* share is TRUE. That'll build up your rep not just as someone who has secret information, but someone whose information is accurate. (You need to be careful about *how much* gossip you share – you don't want to develop a reputation as someone who can't keep a secret!)

That said, it seems to matter LESS if your gossip is <u>true</u>, than if other people LIKE HEARING IT.

That's a **BIG** part of how and why fake news spreads so easily. Another big part is that every time a story gets shared, people use their own words. And that can turn a silly story meant as a joke into a maybe-true story that people take seriously...

As long as each person in the chain hears the story from a friend – someone they trust – they might feel it's OK to share the story *wherever and however they like*.

FAKE NEWS FACT

The more we hear a story, the *more likely* we are to come to trust it – even if it is a **LIE**. This can happen even with an *obviously* false claim, such as

> **" The Moon is made of cheese. "**

If you see this claim *again* and *again* and *again* – even if you hear it from people you hate, or websites you don't trust – there's part of your brain that starts to niggle at you, saying that there **might just be some truth in there**.

It *helps* if the lie is easy to remember – it makes it *harder* if it's complicated. The truth is often complicated.

What's the Moon actually made of?

It's several layers of thick dusty rocks called regolith, on top of hardened volcanic rock called megaregolith.

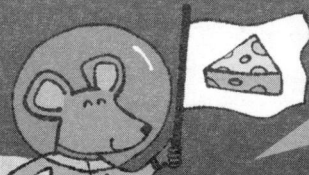

Good luck remembering that!

The inconvenient truth

The author Mark Twain is credited with saying:

> "Never let the truth get in the way of a good story."*

A 'news' article doesn't need to be factual to go viral, it just needs *enough people* to find it interesting or believable enough to share around social media. Sadly, it's often the most extreme or sweeping claims that stand out and gain the most attention online.

> Mainstream news outlets can be slower to get the news out due to the fact-checking process. Non-mainstream websites can take advantage of this, and get their inaccurate version out first.

*No one knows if he definitely said this.

I agree... I agree... I agree...

Social media apps are able to track the articles you stop and read, and use this information to suggest similar articles to you. This can turn your feed into an (**echo chamber**), where you become surrounded by people who all think like you. You all read similar articles, resulting in the version of the news you see online becoming *filtered* and *narrowed*.

> It's amazing how EVERYONE shares my opinion these days. I'm obviously right about everything.

The bigger your echo chamber or 'bubble' becomes, the louder its voice, and then you might start to think that *your opinion* is what *everyone* thinks.

> I second that.

Our brains are great at filling in gaps

We humans don't rely on other people for *everything*. We also have to think for ourselves quite often.

Our brains use a lifetime of experience and knowledge to **fill in any gaps** in our information with a best guess.

OK, I think I can work this out myself...

This covers *everything* – from what we see and hear around us, to what we read, or videos we watch, and stories we hear. The information we fill the gaps with is *often* correct – but not always. This is how many optical illusions work.

What do you see here? Two triangles?

Look again! There are no triangles...

The way our brains fill in gaps is something journalists and advertisers RELY on when writing catchy headlines. But someone who wants to sell fake news can use the same trick to make you THINK something's being said, that is not *actually* being said.

This front page is, potentially, presenting two facts.

It DOESN'T SAY the two things are linked.

Because of the human desire to fill in gaps, most people reading the front page will, in their heads, *automatically* pop in a little "so", thinking that there's a <u>connection between the two statements</u>.

Immigration is up, SO crime is up.

And sometimes, that's what a newspaper editor, politician or disinformer *wants you to think*.

Does the story match your point of view?

Sometimes, when people say they "don't trust the news", it's because they don't agree with a particular news *source*. If the same words came from a source they DO agree with, they'd be more likely to trust it. Especially if the story appears to be confirming something that they already think is true.

Haha 'maxismymate', you are so right. It's been a tough week, but I really appreciate my fans' support after *The Pigeon Today* totally trashed me. We're just regular people! But they won't keep us down.

Gamingdaze

Yeah, I don't bother with the news sites anymore. It's all rubbish. WE LOVE YOU @maX.GameController!

Check this out — here's a link to a way better news site, 'YouKNOWit'. They've investigated loads of these outrageous (smear campaigns) — it's not just me who's got stitched up. Have a read and a share. **POWER TO THE PEOPLE!**

And finally — our brains struggle with intense stress

Psychologists have found, time and again, that almost everything in life is tougher when you're *unwell* or *very stressed*. The bits of our brains that help us to be sociable, figure out who to trust, or to fill in the gaps in what our senses tell us, simply don't function as well when we're seriously STRESSED, ANXIOUS, LONELY or DEPRESSED.

In fact, a common factor linking people who get caught up in disinformation, is that when they started believing it they were *under a lot of stress.**

*You can see references for this on page 174.

Back to Max Green...

maX.GameController

Hey Ajay, just wanted to say THANK YOU for reaching out to me! It's been tough coping with the haters after that Pigeon Today article. Your post suggesting I donate the ad money to charity was genius! So glad to have a new friend on my side!!

AjayJONES (Y_K_it)

Hey Max, no problem. Thank *YOU* for the mention this week. It's bringing in big numbers. BTW we've got a heads up about a new Government Policy...

maX.GameController

Oh wow, there's MORE?? I'll make sure to check in with YouKNOWit every day, and keep my fans in the know!!

Think like a SCHEMER

Now it's time to take a step over to 'The Dark Side'. Imagine that YOU want to create shockwaves online, dividing popular opinion with some propaganda.

What tricks could you use in your article?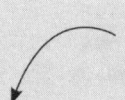

- **Keep it simple.**
  If you can fit a story into a single headline, so much the better.

- **Make it feel personal.**
  This can be as simple as putting the word 'you' into a story. People respond more to stories that directly affect them.

- **Make it intriguing.**
  Don't try to tell the whole story. Leave the reader with questions, so they can fill in the gaps with their own speculation.

Make someone feel as if they're learning a **secret**, so they can show off to their friends that they heard it first.

> How do you STOP falling for fake news, then?

Rule #1

STOP before you share! No matter where you hear a news story, even from your best friend or parents, *don't just forward it, think about it.* Maybe check it on a news website you trust to confirm if the story really <u>is</u> true, and to *get more details*.

Rule #2

If the story seems to have an **agenda**, for example to persuade you to turn against a person, or to side with a political movement, *be suspicious!*

Rule #3

If you keep hearing the same story *over and over*, but only on social media and NOT on any TV or radio news channels, *be suspicious!*

> Something's fishy here...

Let's test your brain...

1. Which line is LONGER?

a) ⟵⟶

b) ⟩―――⟨

2. Your social media feed keeps telling you that teleportation has just been invented, but it's not on mainstream media anywhere...

a) You trust your GUT – it's fake news!
b) You trust your feed. After all, the same story keeps being shared by your friends.
c) It's a joke, obviously.

3. Your friend-group chat shares a story about a classmate – he was seen shoplifting. Do you:

a) Share the story wider – it's great gossip!
b) Keep it to yourself, it's none of your business.
c) Challenge your friends on the group chat to find out if the story is actually TRUE.

Answers:

1. They're the SAME LENGTH. Check with a ruler. Even if you know this optical illusion already, your brain can't help but tell you that line 'b' MUST be longer. It's the sort of trick fake news-makers love.
2. It's FAKE NEWS. Any invention THAT wild would be on the news everywhere. Perhaps it started as a joke, but what's the punchline?
3. There's no correct answer. But you might learn something about yourself by seeing what <u>your own</u> instinctive reaction was...

Chapter
3

Reaching a wide audience

What do adverts and fake news have in common?
They both want to **GRAB YOUR ATTENTION!**

Advertisers are skilled at reaching an audience. Some of the tools and techniques they use to do this, such as content (**algorithms**), are also employed by those who spread fake news.

Really successful marketing messages are so subtle, they simply give us a 'gut feeling' we should buy something. Carefully chosen phrases and imagery can have more of an effect on you – even in passing – than you might think.

Adverts all around

To maximize sales, advertisers are careful to place their ads where lots of people will see them, such as football stadiums or on public transport. Just like hearing the same radio jingle over and over, the more times you see an ad, the more likely you are to remember the product – and to believe whatever claims the ad makes...

MADE YOU LOOK!

CONGRATULATIONS! You have been chosen to receive a **FREE** laptop 180! CLICK HERE TO CLAIM YOUR FREE GIFT

STAY COOL SHADES! 30% off! one day only Sign up TODAY! HURRY! Limited Stock! Click here

YOUR GYM NEEDS YOU! NOW OR NEVER - UNBEATABLE OFFERS CLICK THIS LINK

Adverts and headlines have attention-grabbing wording, in a **BIG FONT**. Common words that appeal to us include:

!!! **NOW** **FREE** **PROVEN TO** **NEW** **GUARANTEED** **EASY** !!! **BETTER THAN** **QUICK**

Adverts may use the words '*HURRY!*' or '*LAST FEW*' to make you feel like you need to buy quickly before other people do.

Setting the (click) bait

Advertisers need to decide where the best places are to advertise online, to get as many views as possible. This is why you'll see adverts IN THE WAY while you scroll your social media feed. They also sometimes pop-up while you're reading something online.

You might think it's easy to ignore these *obvious* online adverts – until the fascinating headline of an article jumps out at you...

FAMOUS SINGER MADE THESE THREE OUTRAGEOUS DEMANDS...

FIVE SECRETS TO EXAM SUCCESS TEACHERS DON'T WANT YOU TO KNOW!

These headlines are formatted to make the *dramatic* words **STAND OUT**.

You'd think they'd keep it short and snappy to get your attention, but often the headlines are long enough that you can't quite see the full thing... making you even more likely to click on it!

> **DAYTIME TV PRESENTER SO EMBARRASSED TO REVEAL REAL...**

> **A-LIST HOLLYWOOD ACTOR HORRIFIED BY SON'S...**

Attention-grabbing headlines like this are called **clickbait**, and they're used to direct you to a website full of adverts desperate to get your eyeballs on them.

Getting you hooked

Clickbait articles are not necessarily fake stories, but it's good to be aware of why websites create them. To prove they are popular enough for advertisers to invest in, websites need to keep you on their site for as long as possible.

They want to keep you scrolling for hours,* watching videos, clicking and sharing links – because while *you're* doing *that*, they're making money from the ad space they've sold.

Social media apps also host adverts, and they use **cookies** and algorithms to make sure you see adverts most relevant to you.

I... just... can't... look away.

*It's true – around 1 in 5 people in the UK spend more than **5 hours a day** scrolling social media.

Cookies

A website cookie is a little file of information, a bit like a digital sticky note. It's generated and stored on your device as you browse a website. Cookies can do things such as remember your login details for a site. Useful stuff.

Some websites allow 'third-party' cookies to be generated on their site. These are paid for by advertisers, and they make a note of what you look at on the website.

Third-party cookies can also note how you move from one website to another. They track the links you click on. Clever! Advertisers use this info about your *interests* and *shopping habits* to target you with adverts relevant TO YOU.

You CAN disable most cookies through a pop-up, though sometimes you can't help leaving a trace of your online activity.

Honestly, I buy ONE hat for one party and now the internet thinks I'm obsessed with hats.

Pick us!

Choose me!

Feeding the algorithm

You only have to look up the new trainers your mate has... and *uncannily*, two minutes later an advert pops up, like it read your mind.

Advertisers can feed all this data on what people *search for*, and then go on to *buy*, into computer programs called **algorithms**. These predict other products that people like you – who like these trainers – might also want.

> ANY information you put online is data that can be **sold** by the website to advertisers, to use for targeted advertising.

This includes information on social media. For example, if you reveal your *age* and *where you live* on your profile, then you'll see ads aimed at people your age, in your area.

Social media algorithms will track ANYTHING you click on - including 'news' articles - in order to show you similar things.

That means that even if you dismiss something you've read as fake news, you *might* fall for the next article that pops up. It's all too easy for algorithms to lead you down a path of disinformation.

Spreading the word

Advertisers always want a 'buzz' around their advert or product, from rapid word-of-mouth recommendations. So they may also offer incentives such as **special discounts** to customers if they recommend the product to their friends, because people tend to *trust* and *value* their friends' recommendations.

As well as their friends, social media users increasingly trust the opinions and views of online influencers, whose recommendations appear 'natural'.

Influencers who have a large number of **followers** or **subscribers** are very attractive to advertisers because if they recommend a product, that endorsement will reach lots of people quickly. Some influencers are *paid* by advertisers, or given valuable freebies, to recommend a product...

This can create a kind of fake news, where you *think* a recommendation is genuine when it may not actually reflect the influencer's real feelings. This is called **stealth marketing** because it's not always obvious that it's happening.

Sticking to the rules

When you know you're watching or looking at an advert, you're more likely to be sceptical of what you're being told. Stealth marketing, however, can catch you off your guard. Especially when you're hearing from an influencer you like and trust.

Some countries have strict rules about influencer recommendations to avoid people being misled in this way. Many countries require influencers to mark their sponsored content with **ad** or .

There are (**regulatory bodies**) such as the Advertising Standards Agency (ASA) in the UK, that make rules about what *can* and *can't* appear in an advert. They monitor and investigate complaints about adverts or stealth marketing.

The most popular influencers – such as our fictional Max Green – are **so trusted** that what they say holds a lot of power – or *influence*. Their opinions could be misinterpreted as fact, and may easily lead to misinformation...

Think like an INFLUENCER

Back to 'The Dark Side'!

Imagine **YOU** are an influencer and you've been sent loads of free products to push. What techniques would you use to try to make them stand out, and to get your followers to buy, BUY, **BUY**?

> Here's an even bigger challenge: make a product **GO VIRAL**.
>
> Would you dare try any of THESE techniques?

- You could LIE about how good the product is, or how bad rival products are. (Beware – your followers might not trust you in the future.)

- Use phrases such as 'up to' and 'less than' – few will notice that they are virtually meaningless.

- See if you can find some influencer friends to recommend the product, too. Share your freebies – for a favour.

- BOTS are your friend! You can get bots to flood social media talking about your product.

- People HATE missing out. Anything you can do to make people have an opinion – ANY opinion – will get them chatting about these products.

- TIME LIMITS are another great tactic. Make followers believe that NOW is the best time to buy, or they'll miss out on the best deal.

Real influencers have used ALL OF THESE TRICKS – even the one about lying – and many more.

You're probably so used to advertising that you think it's easy to ignore, and that YOU don't get influenced by the algorithm. Good for you. But...

...ask yourself these questions:

- When you need to buy something – from a sports top to a toothbrush – how often do you opt for a brand you've heard of, or your friends use, as opposed to something totally new?

- When you last wrote a gift wishlist, how many of the items on it had you seen recommended somewhere online?

- If advertising is so easy to ignore, why do companies spend SO MUCH MONEY on it?

Chapter 4

What's the angle?

Adverts have an agenda – they want to sell you something. But politicians' speeches or certain news articles *also* have an agenda, which can be harder to spot. Those who want to convince people to share their view, will use language to appeal to people's **emotional, less rational side**.

Persuasive campaigns hope that if they can convince you *emotionally* first, then your mind will follow. They do this using powerful imagery and memorable wording.

Painting a picture

You might see video ads online for charities or political campaigns. They often involve an **emotional scenario**, which the makers hope you will feel an instant connection to. This makes it more likely that the video will stay in your mind after it's over.

Images and voiceovers might use physical metaphors – such as 'climbing a mountain', implying effort and progress to overcome an obstacle – to make the story feel engaging and realistic.

making it personal

Because I'm worth it.

RADICAL

Because you're worth it.

ATTAINABLE

Because we're worth it.

INCLUSIVE

In 1971, beauty brand L'Oréal came up with a slogan for an expensive new hair dye.

This idea that a woman could spend **her own money** as she liked was a strong feminist message at the time.

Since then, the slogan has subtly changed to make sure the product still feels relevant.

> Even though the wording of the slogan subtly changes, the original feminist message was so POWERFUL and MEMORABLE that people still identify with it, and the L'Oréal brand.

Getting it out there

If an advertiser's or influencer's video engages enough people, it could go viral. This means it's shared and forwarded by many people, spreading far and wide across the internet.

Everyone should see this!

Before you know it, the content is so familiar you could quote it in your sleep, and the content-creators have achieved their goal.

...ChooChoo Chocs, the treat you want, the treat you deserve...

News reporters ALSO want to reach the largest audience. Nowadays, most people find out what's going on in the world from news websites or social media, rather than a printed newspaper.

The *advantage* of people reading verified news online, for reporters and readers, is that news can spread and be updated quickly. The *disadvantage* for reporters and readers is that **FAKE news can spread just as quickly...**

Where news and advertising meet

News reporting is FACTUAL. People expect what they see and read in the news to be the truth. But different things can influence what gets reported and how. For example, some mainstream news outlets such as:

- newspapers
- magazines
- radio stations
- websites
- social media platforms

may be funded, like many websites, by ads;

advertisers PAY news outlets to display their adverts.

This relationship can work well... until an advertiser objects to a news story. For example, a car manufacturer could threaten to pull their advertising from a paper if it runs an article about increases in car accidents.

Run that story and we advertise elsewhere.

Other considerations

Something to bear in mind when reading a newspaper or a news website is that you might see some articles **that are NOT news reports...**

Things that aren't 'the news':

OPINION PIECES, or **COLUMNS** – these are written by journalists who voice their views on certain subjects.

SATIRICAL ARTICLES – these look realistic but are often written in a sarcastic tone, making fun of topical issues in the news.

ADVERTORIALS – these are a combination of an editorial article and an advert. They might be written by a publicist or a journalist, but they will feature a brand's name and logo and speak highly of them, similar to a positive review.

PRESS RELEASES – these are articles written by marketing departments. Like advertorials, they are promotional material, containing information about a product or brand. They talk about upcoming events and can have a slight story angle to sound more like news, such as mentioning:

STARS FROM LATEST SUPERHERO BLOCKBUSTER TO WED
– OUT NOW AT LOCAL CINEMAS!

That sort of thing...

> These things aren't pretending to be news! But a snippet of 'news' shared on social media, might, in fact, be from one of these articles.

FILLERS

Mainstream news outlets need to publish articles all the time, for advertisers to put ads in. Sometimes, if there isn't enough daily news to write about, they write articles *just to fill the space.* These are known as **fillers**. They look harmless and light, with catchy headlines.

It's National Kiss a Frog Day!

I've been searching my pond for a little green prince, but no luck yet.

Pondlife expert Rush Reed says it's the best time to see them, so get those glasses on.

Make sure you send us your photos and we'll…

Often, fillers are about something related to science, nature, the climate, economics – *anything that changes regularly enough* to pass as news. And advertisers can get in on this too.

For example, ice cream makers could sponsor (pay for) a science 'news' story, about how tastebuds can't tell the difference between ice cream flavours. With a (**soundbite**) from an expert thrown in to give some credibility, they can create a filler piece that gets people thinking about how *they'd really like some ice cream right now...*

Smart senses

Think you can tell your caramel from your vanilla? Think again!

Scientists have confirmed that it's our NOSES that tell us which is which. Mmm, smells like summer!

SPONSORED BY YUMMY-YUM ICES

Presenting the story

Journalists choose the most important elements of a news story to write about, and what the headline should be. This choice of how to write the story is called the **angle**, and it depends on what they think their readers would like to know. Journalists are employed by, or sell their stories to, news outlets, who choose the stories they run.

Editorial opinion can make a big difference to how the same piece of news is presented and interpreted all over the world. Freelance journalists – who are their own boss – may write up the same piece of news with different angles, depending on who wants to buy their story.

In many countries, certain news sites are **politically affiliated**, which means they support one political party or set of ideas. Their news stories will be written from their *preferred political angle*, and they will be <u>selective</u> about the news stories they publish, e.g. only publishing the positive stories about a political party, and ignoring anything negative. Those who are not (**impartial**) are (**biased**), which means they lean towards one particular opinion at the expense of all the facts.

> How do you know the particular bias of a source?

> It's not always obvious. It's something adults learn over time, but we all have our own biases (even if we're not aware of them!). One person might believe a newspaper is very sensible, while another might think the same paper is outrageous.

Doing the dirty work

Sometimes news stories are published to achieve a specific goal, or agenda. A celebrity, politician or other public figure may become the focus of a smear campaign, which is the deliberate spread of NEGATIVE STORIES about their past, 'dug up' in order to ruin their reputation or make them appear less trustworthy.

Celebrity dumps "cheat" politician

V

Politician denies being linked with "loser" celebrity

Scandal sells, and if there isn't a juicy enough story to dig up, the site or newspaper can get away with *implying* one with a carefully placed question mark and a vague photo.

Any statements of denial from the celebrity add interest to the story...

Hey! This never happened!

Well, there's no smoke without fire!

...and the news site gets MORE eyeballs and advertising money.

How to turn it around –
AKA PUTTING A POSITIVE SPIN ON IT

Political figures and celebrities employ people to manage their public image. Often this job involves (spin) - presenting negative information or news about an event in a better light.

Right, we'll start by saying it was a difficult decision and cushion it with some praise...

Spin is a subtle way of **influencing public opinion**. And it can take many forms, from deflecting aspects of the story onto someone seen as less trustworthy, to 'reframing the narrative'. That means, changing the focus to something POSITIVE about the person instead.

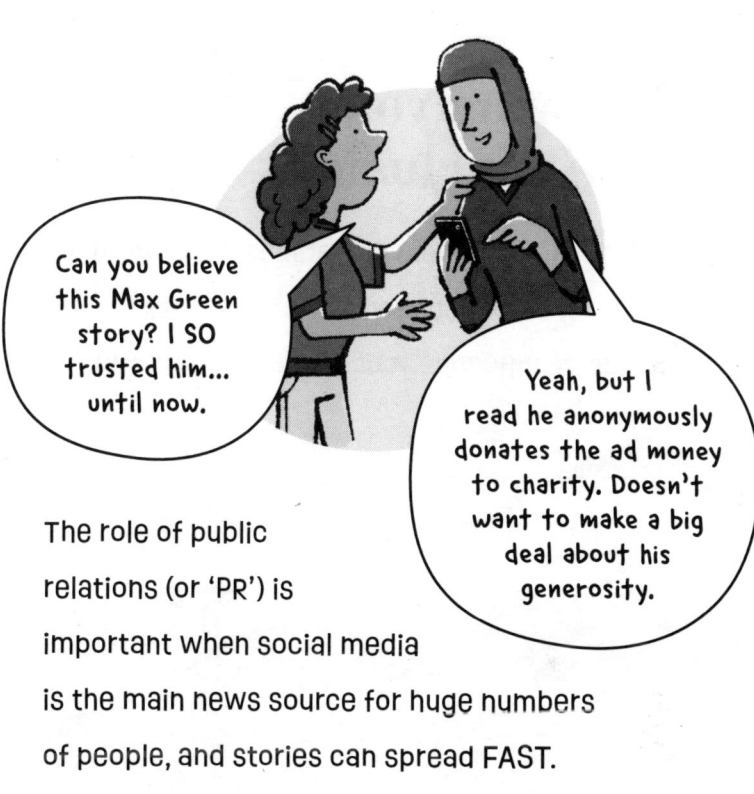

Can you believe this Max Green story? I SO trusted him... until now.

Yeah, but I read he anonymously donates the ad money to charity. Doesn't want to make a big deal about his generosity.

The role of public relations (or 'PR') is important when social media is the main news source for huge numbers of people, and stories can spread FAST. People who can control how a story is presented online have a lot of **power** if their version of the story comes out on top, becoming popular enough to *look like* the truth. (Prejudice) and **impulsiveness** can lead people to forward articles before they've stopped to consider and fact-check them, which increases the circulation of fake news.

Drawing your own conclusions

Biased media outlets sometimes write articles implying a link between two unconnected things, to influence your opinion. For example:

STAY SAFE! DITCH THE SUNSCREEN! As sunscreen sales increase, so does the risk of painful jellyfish encounters.

The writers of this article want you to *infer* that wearing sunscreen causes jellyfish stings.

Does it?

Actually, it's WARM WEATHER that makes people buy sunscreen, and increases the number of people in the sea. The two facts are linked only by a third **variable** – warm weather – <u>one doesn't cause the other</u>. Jellyfish aren't attracted to the smell of sunscreen.

> **Bias in imparting information** can pave the way for **prejudice in interpreting it**. Someone might read this article and think, ah yes, those who sell sunscreen have been putting our safety at risk all these years for the sake of profit. How many millions of people have been fooled by them!

A *totally inaccurate* article like this could be **sponsored** by a handy advert for aftersun – something you need to buy when you've got sunburned from not wearing sunscreen!*

> Best spread the word and boycott sunscreen brands.

*And that is MUCH RISKIER than paddling in the sea.

Is it ALL just angles?

The short answer is... "YES". Lots of news sites, and websites such as Wikipedia, try REALLY HARD to be un-biased, and only report verifiable facts. But everyone who works on any website is human, meaning they can't help but have biases. Even the non-human AIs and algorithms people use were programmed and trained by humans, and are liable to make the same mistakes (sometimes worse).

The longer – and happier! – answer is: **IT DOESN'T MATTER**. Yes, news sites, politicans, advertisers and even influencers all have some sort of agenda. Learning to see through the angles is like getting used to how your friends talk differently. It comes with time and practice.

THE GOOD NEWS

Although mainstream news outlets can be biased, and have an angle, you can still trust that the FACTS they present ARE FACTS.

> ### Here's how they verify a story:
>
> When one journalist says they have some news, someone else has to check it from at least one, usually two, other sources. This might be an eyewitness of a major event, or a politician who was personally at a big meeting.

Even biased news outlets use this system. The FACTS of the story don't change from one news outlet to the next, just the way the story is presented, and *which* facts are included.

Your friends and your social media feeds don't have to verify news. **Trust THEM at your own risk...**

Getting the story straight

We humans have a desire for certainty. Uncertainty can make us feel uncomfortable, so we look for information we feel we can rely on and trust.

The truth IS here somewhere.

It's pretty normal to check a few weather forecasts rather than relying on just one, to see if there is a (**consensus**). But it's also a good habit to visit more than one news outlet to see if different versions of the same story match up.

If we can't find a **consensus** on a news story, or we feel reporters are holding information back, that can make us uncertain and distrustful. Mainstream news is constantly updated though, so keep checking back to learn more on the story. Sometimes a healthy (scepticism) turns into **PARANOIA** that you can't *ever* trust the media. This can push people to websites that promote 'alternative facts' (conspiracy theories) instead...

Aargh! I just can't find a consensus in here.

Is **truth** stranger than **fiction**?

Conspiracy theories are born when people spot inconsistent information across news stories, or find a gap in the information. People don't like to feel that they are being manipulated by the media, so they put their trust instead in what individual people are saying.

As always, I trust your judgement!

Even a stranger who is 'just like us' saying

" this happened to me "

helps us to relate to and trust a story.

Conspiracy theorists like to gain attention by saying something *different to the mainstream*. They present themselves as an average person who has discovered a **national lie**, so that they can turn a news story into a NEW story – one they can control.

Success! Now what else can I do with this fame and power...?

Remember not to fall for someone else's agenda.

Tread carefully when you come across someone claiming to 'expose the truth'. Swimming against the tide of popular opinion ISN'T THE SAME as telling the truth – especially when getting noticed online can lead to making money online.

££££ **FROM ADVERTISERS**

££££ **FROM TV INTERVIEWS**

££££ **CROWDFUNDED FROM FANS**

Meanwhile, the latest with Max Green...

Hey everyone, Max Green here.

Shout out to all my new followers! You're right about 'Dino Swim' — too glitchy. Give it a miss.

Ci11ian_C00ps
Max! Your videos are GREAT. So glad I saw those articles about you. I was looking for a new gaming channel. I'm subscribed!

In other news, my friends at YouKNOWit just gave me a heads-up. The government's planning to CANCEL mobile phone insurance! Luckily they've got a plan...

Gamingdaze

What!!!! No way? Good job you're in the know, Max. Can't trust the government to tell us anything.

To keep your phone protected before the big switch-off, use this voucher code for 25% off at TreasURfone — link on YouKNOWit. You give them all your info, and they take care of the rest. Whew! Back to gaming!

Think like a CONSPIRACY THEORIST

Imagine YOU want plenty of views of the new website you've set up. Maybe you could make a name for yourself creating a bizarre theory to get people's attention...

Take a look at this example:

< DODGE THE GREEN SQUARES IN GROWBLOX GAMES >

Did you know, every time your GROWBLOX character steps onto a green square in an 'obby' game, you're giving $0.0001 to a secret bank account? These games are super addictive, and now you know why!

Here's your 'box of tricks'...

Use grains of truth

A lie is easier to sell if it's at least **partly true**. It IS often true that simply by playing a game, someone somewhere is getting a tiny amount of money – from ads. Certain buttons can lead to an ad site, which means another hit of money.

Make it shareable

The headline practically begs you to **share** this 'secret knowledge' with your friends. It helps that it's all about a game – something you and your friends like.

Leave questions unanswered

This story doesn't say **where** the money comes from, or **who** the bank account belongs to. If people are motivated to find that out for themselves, you KNOW you've **got them hooked**.

Leave them wanting MORE

The most successful conspiracy theories **aren't just a single story**. They're more like a soap opera, where people uncover – and share – more new 'truths' every day.

> OMG! The Green Square con runs on NiteFort too! How far back does this go??

News story, advertorial — or just plain nonsense?

Read this story, then note down any parts that seem a bit... 'off'.

Summer's SECRET PERIL: Ice cream

A recent study has revealed a link between ice cream and sunburn. "I've seen kids smearing ice cream on their cheeks like it's sunscreen," said one coffee-hut staff member, an eye-witness to the sunburn epidemic. "Everyone knows a nice HOT DRINK actually cools you down better than a mushy ice cream."

Did you spot these red flags? There may be many more, as this is a TOTALLY MADE-UP story.

1. **"A recent study"** – which study? Who by?
2. **"has revealed a link"** – what link? Is it just that in summer, more people buy ice cream, AND more people get sunburn?
3. **"everyone knows"** – DOES everyone know? Is this a fact? A handy claim for a coffee shop in summer...
4. **You could query the WHOLE ARTICLE.** Is it actually reporting news? It's very light on details.

Chapter
5

Facts v figures

People who want to persuade you to share an opinion may well use **statistical data** - a percentage, fraction or an average - to help to gain your trust. Numbers have a way of making something made-up sound more 'true'...

Percentages and averages can make a claim believable, regardless of what those numbers actually ARE. They may imply that scientific research has PROVEN something, which could persuade you that believing the claim is a *rational* and *informed* decision.

8 out of 10

78%

Statistics are a GREAT tool to identify trustworthy facts. But there are people who use them to persuade others that something SEEMS true, even if it's not. The main trick they use is to *keep things as simple as possible*, which can result in statistics being taken out of context or presented in a confusing way. This chapter covers six ways statistics can be used to LOOK trustworthy, whilst misleading people:

3/4

Using the term 'on average'
Scaling up numbers
Cherry-picking data
Manipulating words
Manipulating pictures
Ignoring proportions

① Using the term 'on average'

A common term that people are familiar with and often gets quoted in the news is 'on average'.

Did you know... ...there are actually <u>three</u> types of average:

Calculating an average

- To calculate a **mean** average, you *add up* all the numbers, and then *divide* by the number of numbers.

- The **median** average is the *middle number* in an *ordered* set of numbers.

- The **mode** average of a set of numbers is the number that comes up *most frequently*.

Which average?

> **Different types** of average produce **different results**.

For example, about these families...

...ALL of these statements are true:

a) The average family size is <u>three children</u>.

b) The average family size is <u>two children</u>.

c) The average family size is <u>one child</u>.

> Three different averages, yet **all true? HOW?**

Look back at the family groups on the previous page to check these facts:

- The **mean** number of children in a family **is 3**.

- The **median** number of children in a family **is 2** (just as many families have fewer than 2 children as have more than 2).

- The **mode** (the most common) number of children in a family **is 1**.

So, remember...

Writers of persuasive articles and adverts can choose <u>whichever average best suits their argument or claim</u>. This may end up misleading consumers, especially if it's not clear in an advert or article which type of average has been used.*

*Advertisers only want to use whichever average sounds best.

Hot, hotter, hottest

The temperatures used on these holiday posters are *mean* averages, which is the **most commonly used** average. (It's more likely to result in a number to at least one decimal point, which sounds accurate, reliable and scientific.)

Looking closer

Whichever type of average you are calculating, you have to start with a **data set**, which is the *collection of numbers* you are looking at.

Each table below is a data set. The **data range** is the *spread of numbers in each set*, from highest to lowest.

JUNE temperatures in °C

TROPICA

1	2	3	4	5	6
18	21	26	18	21	23
7	8	9	10	11	12
18	22	25	29	32	37
13	14	15	16	17	18
36	37	38	40	42	41
19	20	21	22	23	24
36	34	29	26	24	18
25	26	27	28	29	30
18	23	25	22	20	20

SCORCHIO

1	2	3	4	5	6
20	21	21	22	22	26
7	8	9	10	11	12
23	25	28	29	32	30
13	14	15	16	17	18
29	31	32	30	32	30
19	20	21	22	23	24
32	31	32	30	29	28
25	26	27	28	29	30
27	26	24	24	21	20

Choosing wisely

If you just look at the **mean** temperatures for the two destinations (27.3° for Tropica and 26.9° for Scorchio), you might think they're pretty similar. But as the tables show, there's actually a big difference between the *range* of temperatures for each destination. Comparing the **mode*** temperatures (18° for Tropica; 32° for Scorchio), is more useful.

To make a decision like this, what you really want to know is not what's *average*, but what is MOST COMMON, or USUAL.

Can I change my mind please?!

*The mode average of a set of numbers is the number that comes up most frequently.

2. Scaling up numbers

Sometimes a headline statistic has been *scaled up* from a smaller **sample**. For example, this researcher is doing a survey, recording the family size of everyone they meet in a play park over the course of one day.

I'll just scale up my sample data to show average family sizes for the whole population.

The researcher did the exact same study the previous year. These are the results:

	Last year	This year
Mean average	3 children	2 children
Median average	2 children	2 children
Mode average	1 child	2 children

The researcher could choose to use these results to write a news article with either of these completely opposite headlines:

*

> Notice the median average family size hasn't changed, but that's not much of a news story.

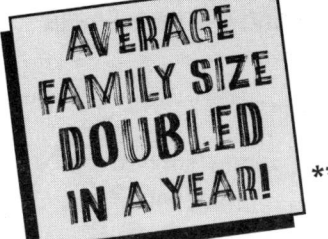**

*Mean last year v mean this year.
**Mode last year v mode this year.

The total number of children in this sample is far too small to scale up to a population of millions in a country, which means the sample data is <u>not representative</u>; it's inaccurate.

If the *sample size* and the *type of average used* weren't mentioned in the story, that would also make it misleading – readers would assume that the data behind the headline is accurate, and it isn't.

> And that's even if the article writers are honest enough to be comparing <u>the same type</u> of average for each year...

3) Cherry-picking data

Sometimes a statistic is cherry-picked from a collection of data, meaning other relevant information is available. For example, in 2007 the UK Advertising Standards Agency (ASA) banned a Colgate toothpaste advert that claimed:

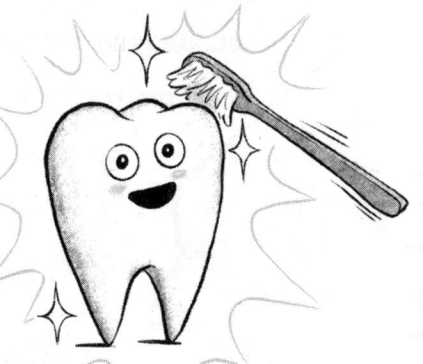

80% of dentists* recommend Colgate.

The ASA said this implied that Colgate was the preferred toothpaste for dentists. Actually, many of the dentists surveyed recommended <u>more than one</u> toothpaste, which meant some other toothpaste brands listed in the survey came out just as popular as Colgate.

*Out of how many? How many dentists were asked? How many responded to the survey?

Colgate cherry-picked the statistic that sounded the best. And if Colgate hadn't come out well at all in the survey, they could have just repeated it with different dentists until they got a result they liked!

This way of playing around with survey data isn't untrue, but it is **misleading**.

Cherry-picking data is also a way to angle a science or political news story to suit an agenda.

Remember...

The CONTEXT for a statistic — where it came from and what it can be compared against — is as important as the number itself.

Don't automatically trust a headline that uses an eye-catching statistic. Without context, statistics can be next to USELESS.

> To be confident in the stats, check the sources!

4 Manipulating words

The words accompanying the numbers can present the same facts in different ways. For example:

75% fat-free

sounds better than

only 25% fat.

Sometimes the usefulness of the numbers is purposefully concealed by the wording:

only 7 grams of sugar

or

more than 10% real fruit!

Without a benchmark to compare against, you might not know whether 7 grams or 10% is a lot.

Um, I *think* this yogurt is good for me?

Other vague but positive-sounding phrases include things such as:

- HELPS TO...
- ...AS PART OF A BALANCED DIET
- MAY PREVENT...

making a claim

A brand of superglue or toothpaste may make claims such as **"nothing else is stronger/more effective"**, but that might be because all brands are EQUALLY strong and effective.

Our brand is... just as strong as yours!

Double drama

'Doubling your chances' may sound significant and impressive if it's in relation to playing a lottery. But having *double a 1-in-a-million chance...* still only takes you to a *2-in-a-million chance.*

I've won the lotto!

ZAP

GAK!

If it's double the chance of something HORRIBLE happening, headline-writers can make it sound more dramatic by presenting it as a fraction or percentage. For example, 'risk up **100%**' sounds far more serious than 'risk up from **1 in 100** people to **2 in 100** people'. Yet, they're the SAME THING.

⑤ Manipulating pictures

The way a statistic is presented – as a *number*, a *percentage* or a *fraction* – makes a difference to how it is interpreted. If **ten out of fifteen** people surveyed agreed with something, it could be presented as '**two thirds** of people agreed', which might sound like a larger amount than '**67%** of people agreed', and certainly more than just '**ten** people agreed'.

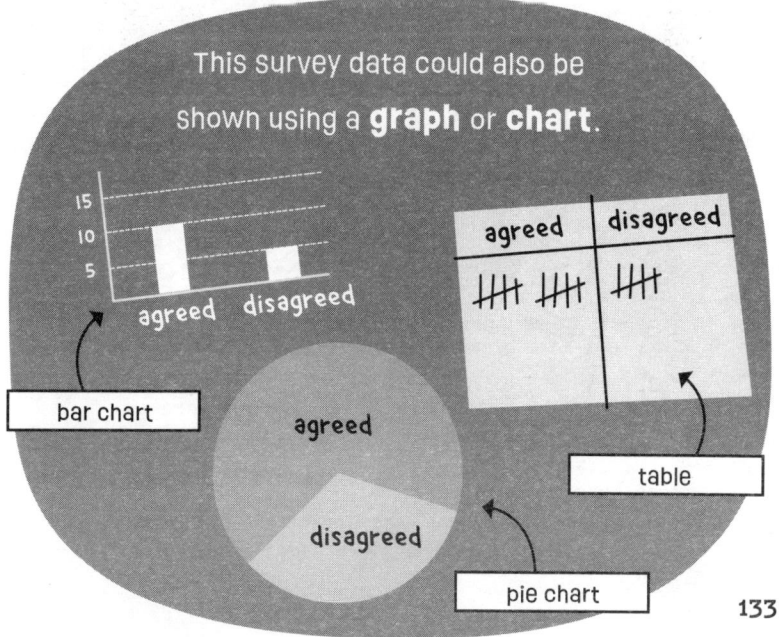

This survey data could also be shown using a **graph** or **chart**.

Often a chart or graph is a more useful way to show statistical information than just a single number, even in context. They show a data range in a visual way to make it easier to understand. Charts and graphs can always reveal more information than a catchy headline.

First year shoe sizes...

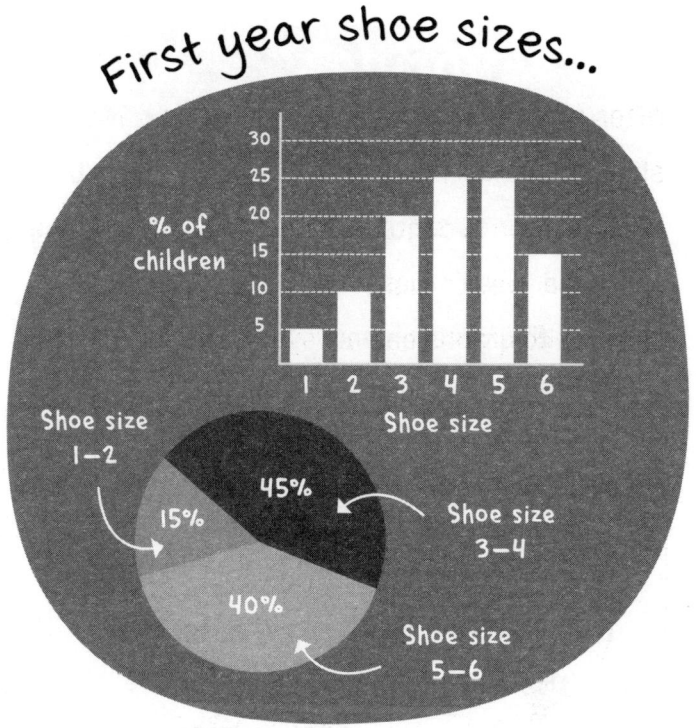

The mean average shoe size might be size 4. *But* these graphs show that the actual distribution of shoe size is pretty even, between a size 3 and size 5 shoe. They also show that *only one quarter* of first year children are likely to fit a size 4 shoe. This is the **context** behind the statistic, showing that one average doesn't fit all.

Ignoring proportions

You'll often see statistics reported in the news in relation to a government policy. Politicians love a statistic, especially if it's a **DRAMATIC** one.

- A common manipulation of a statistic that a political party might use is to claim that cases of CRIME, DISEASE or ANYTHING NEGATIVE (that they can blame on someone else) **ARE UP!** When actually there may just be an increase in <u>reports</u> of these negative things. (Politicians may have asked doctors and police officers to include more <u>types</u> of disease or crimes in their counting, for example.)

- An <u>increase in population size</u> can also affect the way the numbers work. For example, for reported cases of a disease:

> **2 CASES IN A POPULATION OF 100**
>
> is the same as
>
> **6 CASES IN A POPULATION OF 300.**
>
> Yes, CASES HAVE **TRIPLED** – gasp – but...
>
> the population has **ALSO TRIPLED.**
>
> So, the **proportion** of cases actually remains the same.

Nobody panic. You're no more likely to catch this disease than you were before! Phew.

Optical illusions

Sometimes a chart is actually another clever way for political campaigns to **exaggerate** or **manipulate** the truth...

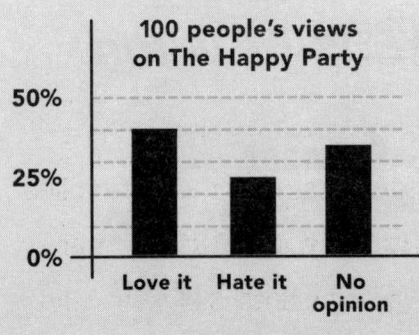

Spot the differences...

Which one grabs your attention more?

The data has been simplified in the second graph:
- The 'hate it' and 'no opinion' categories have been combined into one.
- The larger scale used on the x-axis makes the 'love it' bar look smaller.

This graph makes The Happy Party look less popular.

Size matters

Sometimes it's the *dimensions* on the chart that can be misleading. The chart above implies an amount **significantly increasing** year on year. Actually, when the data is shown using bars instead of an image (as below), there is only a **small difference** between the height of the bars, and therefore the data between the years. The waste-bag picture has increased not just in height but in *width* too, making the increase look far bigger than it really is.

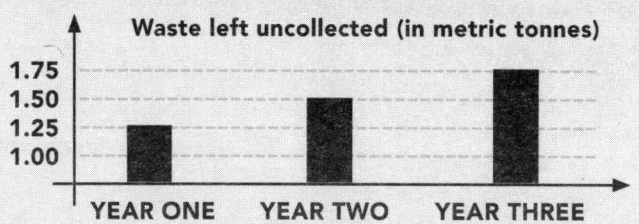

How to spot-check a statistic

Take time to  before you share or comment on a statistic. Ask yourself:

» Does the main message of this article hinge on a statistic or chart?

» Can you think of any other information or context that might be missing?

» Would being able to see a wider data range, or a different type of average, change the message?

» Is there a tiny * somewhere telling you to read some small print?

» When you read the small print, does it answer your questions, or raise more?

Stay sharp

If a statistic doesn't seem reliable or complete after this spot-check, then it's probably worth ignoring. And if one dodgy statistic is all the content-writer has to persuade you, then

DON'T FALL FOR THEIR TRICKS.

Look into my pie charts... ...so swirly and hypnotic.

> There's nothing wrong with numbers themselves, and they can tell you lots.
>
> If someone has used any of the tricks we've shown, you now have the knowledge to help you better understand what the numbers are, or are not, really showing you.

Think like a POLITICIAN

Now you know how easy it is to manipulate people with statistics, it's time to put yourself in someone else's shoes. Imagine YOU are a politician who wants to ban horror comics.

What might you say about THIS survey?

6 out of 10 people say they AGREE with a ban on horror comics for kids.

- "**Most** people agree with the ban."
- "**60%** of people agree with the ban."
- "**3 out of every 5** people agree with the ban."
- "Nearly **two thirds** of people agree with the ban."

All of those staments are **TRUE** — but which will have more impact?

OR, you could try amending the survey yourself.

- Ask more people, to get a bigger number. That often looks more impressive, even if it's the same proportion.
- Or, if you're feeling sneaky, why not find another 10 people who you already know agree with the ban, and ask them what they think.

16 out of 20 people say they agree with the ban.

And for my next trick

Don't be afraid to let people join up the dots — even if the dots are <u>not actually related.</u>

THE BIG NEWS
Kids who read HORROR COMICS get into trouble more often

Aha! Horror comics MAKE kids behave badly.

What you don't want is to get people asking questions.*

*Maybe the link is backwards – kids who get into trouble a lot ALSO like reading comics that are a little bit naughty.

Taking a closer look

Test how much you've learned about different ways charts can bend the truth.

1. Look at this chart. What's it telling you?

Hawksbill turtles (thousands)

a) Turtles have got smaller in the last 50 years.

b) There are fewer turtles now than 50 years ago.

2. What's wrong with this chart?

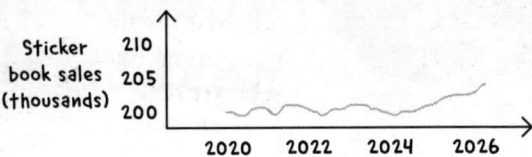

Sticker book sales (thousands)

a) There's nothing wrong with it! But I have a sudden urge to buy more sticker books.

b) The chart is zooming in on a tiny range of sales numbers, to make a small jump look like a big one.

Answers:

1. is b) The chart is ONLY showing numbers of turtles. Using a picture of a turtle, instead of a simple bar, is misleading and might confuse people.

2. is b) Look carefully at the y-axis (on the left). The numbers do not start at zero. It's a trick, to make it look as if the sales increase in 2026 is HUGE.

Chapter
6

Staying ahead of scammers

Fake news unhelpfully gets in the way of real news reporting. It can confuse, upset and divide people. It can *also* be a perfect vehicle for sophisticated, and personal, scams.

DON'T HAVE MOBILE INSURANCE?

You're sunk! Jump aboard for our GOLD standard deal, **half price** this week only.

The government's *TURNING THE TIDE* on phone insurance, so grab this deal *QUICK...*

Online scams take different forms, but they generally aim to **steal your money** or **your personal data**.

Digital pick-pocketing

It's always sensible to avoid using public Wi-Fi, which might have *fewer protections* against hacking than your private network.

Scammers also like to spoof genuine Wi-Fi networks – they set up a fake Wi-Fi hotspot, and, if you connect to it, the scammers can see <u>EVERYTHING you do</u>.

NOW CONNECTED TO
SPOOFNET
WI-FI

Computer-savvy criminals also have a range of 'click this link' scams that install **malware** on your device. Malware programs can perform lots of clever tricks, including *recording your key strokes* to steal login details.

A personal approach

If a scammer learns your login details for your social media, they can take over your account and **lock you out**.

> What do they want with MY profile?

Well, they can use personal details about YOU, such as your date of birth, to apply for documents and accounts in YOUR name. They'll also have access to *all your contacts*: people they can line up for more targeted scams now that they can impersonate someone who your friends trust – **YOU!**

F a k e friends

Sophisticated online scams are all about **faking it**.

When a clever scammer successfully pulls off an **impersonation** of an individual or organization, the scam can go on... and on... AND ON – duping higher numbers of people out of larger and larger amounts of money.

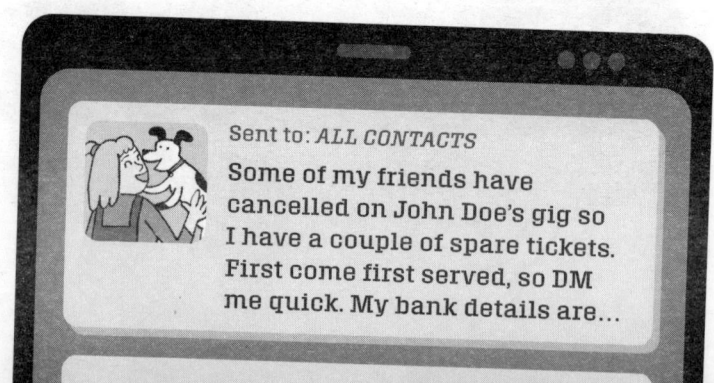

Sent to: *ALL CONTACTS*

Some of my friends have cancelled on John Doe's gig so I have a couple of spare tickets. First come first served, so DM me quick. My bank details are...

Once they are in your account, scammers can set up very convincing-looking **fake webpages**.

The scammer's aim is to **steal** people's credit card details by **FOOLING THEM** into 'donating' to a **fake company**.

Top tips to avoid being caught out by fake communications:

 **DON'T** click on links or call numbers sent via emails, direct messages, texts, or social media.

Instead, search for the official website of the organization to contact them.

 **DON'T** send any donations via bank transfer or money-transfer companies.

If someone asks you to send money to a charity in this way, **DON'T**.

URGENT ACTION REQUIRED!

Criminals impersonating a person, or an organization, in order to steal your money or login details are called 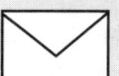 scammers.

They can con huge numbers of people at once by *pretending* to be from reputable companies – copying company logos and email addresses – and sending messages worded to **panic** people into acting *QUICKLY*.

You have 1 new message

FROM: bankinaccountss55@thisbank.com
SUBJECT: You've been hacked!

STAY SAFE

Legitimate companies **won't** ask you to confirm any financial or login details via email.

Check the email address closely – is it misspelled or unusual in any way?

FROM: bankinaccountss55@thisbank.com
SUBJECT: You've been hacked!

THISBANK

Dear Sir,
Your account has been compromised. <u>Click here</u> now to log in and save your account, or call 0990 123 456.

Don't click any links. Go direct to the website and log in from there.

Look the number up on the company's official website, just to be sure.

This all smells rather fishy, don't you think?

AI assistance

Artificial Intelligence (AI) can help scammers write professional-sounding emails. It can also be used for **voice cloning** - `copying a voice` from videos you've uploaded online. It only needs a few seconds of audio to be able to recreate your voice, or the voices of your friends or family. Then the scammer can spoof a phone call, to make it *seem* like it's coming from a real person.

"Darling, I've had my bag stolen and lost all my cards, keys and phone! Please could you send me some money RIGHT NOW, via my PayFriend account, so I can pay for my shopping and a taxi home? And a locksmith..."

Hmm... perhaps I should call Mum on her phone to double check.*

*Yes! You should definitely do that.

Get rich *quick*

Many financial (**fraud**) scams involve persuading people to invest in, or work for, a fake company. Fraud scammers take advantage of people's desire to make more money, by <u>conning them out of the money they already have</u>.

You might see job adverts on social media offering opportunities to make a large amount of money 'quickly and easily' from home: perhaps doing market research, or something else to do with 'marketing'.

GET PAID TO SHOP!

WE NEED YOU!
YOU can get PAID to eat chocolate!
Just sign up for a small fee...

GET RICH QUICK
Learn the secrets. Sign up for only $35 – usually $285!
Places are limited, so be quick!

Also be wary of strangers contacting you online about an exciting 'opportunity' that they have handpicked you for – including offers of modelling jobs.

Such offers often involve a request for a joining or admin fee, or other payment, upfront.

They may also ask you to send identity documents to prove who you are...

...or ask you to call a premium rate number.

These are all **SCAMS**.

Remember – if a job sounds **too good to be true** then it probably is.

Top tips for avoiding money scams

Take time to

 and

» Legitimate companies WON'T ask you to pay them for <u>anything upfront.</u>

» DON'T agree to direct message, or meet up, with <u>anyone you don't know.</u>

» Look up the company website and registered contact details. If YOU call THEM, you can be in control, and be sure of who you're actually speaking to.

FRAUD CASE FILE: TREASURFONE

Months active: **5**
No. of victims: **6,364**
Persons of interest:
**MAX GREEN, AKA MAX.GAMECONTROLLER;
AJAY AND VIV JONES @ YOUKNOWIT**

The long con

Some people **invest** their money in a company or scheme. They hope that at some point in the future this will give them a 'financial return', which means they will get more money back than they put in.

INVEST IN BITCOIN!!
See your money double, triple, increase tenfold in no time!

These kinds of scams can promise anything to *entice people to invest*, often talking up a revolutionary, cutting-edge new product.

Sometimes they pretend to be the kind of company people want to **trust and rely on** - such as an accountancy firm or insurance company.

//MaxxxyG//
Hey, er Ajay, I've had the police round. They're asking about that insurance offer on your website that I was promoting - TreasURfone? Can you call me?

To: AJAYyouKNOWit

Message failed

⚠ AUTO-RESPONSE
This number has not been recognized.

Investment cons are popular with scammers because people **may take a longer time to realize** they have been scammed - giving the criminals plenty of time to make their exit and cover their tracks before the truth comes out.

```
TO:        youknowit@sendmail.com
SUBJECT:   HELLO?
```

Hi Viv, can't get hold of Ajay.
I've sent you guys a few messages...
Could you give me a call? It's about
TreasURfone.

```
FROM:      DoNotReplyautobot@sendmail.com
SUBJECT:   RE: HELLO?
```

This recipient's email address
is invalid.

Once they have collected a large amount of money, the scammers close down the fake website, cut off all contact and DISAPPEAR.

Haha! See ya!

INVALID WEB ADDRESS

THEPIGEONTODAY/.../MAXGREENSTORY

INFLUENCER CHARGED WITH FRAUD

By Jenny J. Bloggs

Gaming influencer **Max Green**, also known as **maX.GameController**, has today been charged in relation to fraudulent financial investment promotions. He was allegedly paid to promote a fake insurance company **'TreasURfone'**, swindling thousands of people. Green also spread rumours about a fictitious banning of mobile insurance by the government, which drove worried victims – desperate to get insurance before a made-up deadline – straight to the fraudsters' website. If convicted, Green could face up to two years imprisonment. His accomplices behind the **'YouKNOWit'** conspiracy website have yet to be traced.

Comment by @SmithsonPete at 13.33PM:
My mate says he didn't do it.

Comment by @DeepFakeJones at 12.04PM:
Whatever. Fake news.

How scam-savvy are you?

Now that you know all about fake news and scam tricks, you won't get any of THESE questions wrong...

...will you?

1) You get a message from an unknown sender, telling you to click on a link to

WIN FREE MONEY

Do you:
a) Click on the link.
b) Report it as spam.

2) You get a phone call from your Mum. It *sounds* like your Mum, but she isn't *talking* like your Mum and she's asking you to urgently send her some money online.

Do you:
a) Send the money.
b) Hang up and try calling your Mum back.

3) Your friend asks to borrow your phone so he can give it to a wannabe hacker that he knows.

> Hey, don't worry, he's a cool guy.

Do you:

a) Give him your phone.
b) Say "No."

4) A stranger stops you on the street, and says you have "the perfect look" for modelling work. They give you a card, and tell you to meet them at some random address with £100 for a photoshoot.

Do you:

a) Meet them at the address with £100 cash.
b) Say "Thanks, but no thanks."

So, how did you do? ???

Did you answer b) for each question? I really hope you did! You've learned the best things to do in those scenarios. If you answered a) at any point, you really should turn back to page 1 and start reading again...

REAL NEWS ALERT: IT'S ALL GOING TO BE OK!

It might seem as if the world – or at least, the internet – is so full of **scams** and **lies** and **deepfakes** that you'll never be able to find the truth.

Don't panic!

The fact is, people love knowing the truth about things, and most of the time, the truth DOES EXIST. Even crooks, scammers and liars need to know facts they can rely on, such as where they are in the world, or what their bank account numbers are.

There will always be ways to determine what's REALLY going on in the world.

This book has also given you lots of reasons to be on your guard, and to be careful who you trust. This can be tiring! Nobody expects you to stop trusting your friends, or to be a perfect reader of news. It's OK if you save up to buy something, only to find you don't enjoy it. It's OK if you accidentally share an old misinformation meme. It's even OK if you fall for fake news from time to time. All you really need to remember is, next time you get an **URGENT** message, or a 'last-chance-to-buy' advert, or see a news headline…

STOP. **THINK.** That's it.

> When you slow down enough, almost everything in life becomes a little bit easier to handle.

GLOSSARY

Words written in *italics* have their own entry.

agenda
a person's real intention or motives. Often hidden within a speech or piece of writing.

algorithm
a series of mathematical instructions, often used to build computer programs that can track a person's likes, and make matching recommendations automatically.

biased
when someone has an unfair opinion for or against a person or idea.

byline
the name(s) of the author and photographer of a news article, and so a way to trace where a story came from.

cherry-picked
when people have ONLY picked the 'best' bits of something. For example, picking the bits of data that suit their point.

clickbait
headlines on the internet designed to make you click on a link to be taken to another page.

consensus
When most people in a group feel they agree on something, they have 'reached a consensus'.

conspiracy theory
an attempt to explain how something in the world REALLY works, usually suggesting that events have been orchestrated or concealed by powerful people. Often, **mainstream media** contradicts these theories.

deepfakes
images, audio or video of someone that has been altered to appear to show them doing or saying something inauthentic.

defamation
a crime when one person deliberately ruins another's reputation, usually by spreading **disinformation**.

disinformation
facts or news that are DELIBERATELY false, often spread by someone with an **agenda**.

echo chamber
when people are surrounded only by other people who have the same opinion, particularly online.

fraud
a crime when one person cheats another out of money by pretending to be someone else, or lying to them.

going viral
when content is shared rapidly across social media.

impartial
when **mainstream media** is impartial, it has no **agenda** beyond reporting the news, and tries not to show any form or **bias** or **prejudice**.

influencer
someone who is able to influence a large number of people on social media, by recommending products and services.

mainstream media
national newspapers, broadcasters and radio stations that are trusted by millions, often run by a major organization.

malware (malicious software)
programs designed to disable, damage or steal data.

misinformation
facts or news that are inaccurate or wrong, usually because they are out of date, or the person providing them has not properly checked the source of the information.

phishing
a cyber attack designed to trick a person into sharing personal information.

polarizing
an opinion or piece of news that is designed to make people on opposite sides of an argument move even further apart.

prejudice
someone's preconceived negative belief about a person, or group, without meeting them. Perhaps based on gossip or *propaganda*, rather than on evidence.

propaganda
a kind of *disinformation*, when a powerful organization – such as a government – spreads false stories about an event, or a group of people, to persuade a population to think one way, and to believe certain false facts.

regulatory bodies
organizations, often run by a government, that enforce rules, such as not making false claims in advertisements.

scepticism
generally assuming something is false or bogus; not trusting things.

smear campaign
when a website or news outlet runs lots of stories designed to ruin the reputation of a person or organization.

smokescreen
when someone tries to hide the truth behind another piece of news.

soundbite
a short phrase that is designed to be played repeatedly on news or audio clips, to catch people's attention and be shared.

spin
phrasing or presenting something so that it seems good, even if it's not really a good thing.

spoof
a fake version of something, usually audio or video, for comedic or criminal purposes.

trolling
posting stories online that are trying to provoke a reaction, usually to make people angry.

verify
to confirm that a person is who they say they are, or that a news story or fact is true.

Index

advertising **12, 67-84, 86-87, 90-95, 103, 127**

Advertising Standards Agency (ASA) **12, 13, 81, 127**

advertorials **92**

agendas **25, 28, 33, 36, 65, 85, 98, 104, 128**

algorithms **73, 76-77, 104**

angles (story) **85-114**

artificial intelligence (AI) **32-33**

averages **115-126, 135**

bias **97, 102-104, 105**

bots **34-35, 83**

brands **12, 84, 92-93, 131**

charts **133-144**

cherry-picking **127-128**

clickbait **21, 72**

conspiracy theories **22-23, 30, 41, 107-109, 112-113**

context **117, 129, 135**

cookies **73-75**

data **76, 115, 122**

deepfakes **32-33, 39, 164**

defamation **35**

disinformation **6, 21-26, 27, 29, 36**

echo chambers **55**

fact-checking **54, 101**

fillers (editorial) **94-95**

fraud **24-25, 154-155, 161**

going viral **38, 54, 83, 88**

governments **27, 136**

graphs **133-144**

Green, Max **12, 13, 60-61, 63, 81, 101, 110-111, 115, 157, 161**

impartiality **97**

impersonation **29, 147-149**

influencers **12, 78-83, 161**

laws **35**

mainstream news **7, 33, 40, 54, 90-91, 94, 105, 107**

malware **146**

media (mainstream) **18, 19, 20**

memes **15, 165**

misinformation **6, 15-20, 36, 81**

MMR vaccine **24-26**

opinion pieces **92**

optical illusions **57, 66, 138-139**

percentages **115, 116, 132-133**

phishing **151**

polarizing **29**

policy (government) **63, 136**

politicians **85, 98, 136**

pop-ups **71, 75**

prejudice **59, 101, 103**

press releases **93**

propaganda **27-31**

psychology/psychologists **39, 43, 62**

public opinion **27, 100**

public relations **101**

regulatory bodies **81**

reputation **37, 48-51, 98**

retractions **25**

satire/satirical **37, 92**

scams **21, 145-163**

smear campaigns **61, 98**

smokescreens **30**

snowball effect **29**

social media **12, 17, 28, 34-35, 54-55, 71, 73, 77, 78, 101, 105**

soundbites **95**

sources **59, 105, 129**

spin **100-101**

sponsors **69, 80, 95, 103**

spoofs **37**

statistics **115-144**

stealth marketing **80-81**

trolling **29**

vaccines **21, 24-26**

verification **7, 21, 33, 105**

voice cloning **153**

Wakefield, Andrew **24-26**

References

Page 39
Elizabeth Loftus carried out her Disneyland-themed study in 2001 at the University of Washington.

Page 42
The Twitter study was led by Soroush Vosoughi at MIT, published in the March 2018 edition of the journal *Science*.

Page 50
A study showing that inaccurate gossip is not always a barrier to trust was led by Miguel Fonseca at the University of Exeter, published in the January 2018 edition of the journal *Games and Economic Behavior*.

Page 62
A study that found a link between stress and conspiracy theories was led by Viren Swami at Anglia Ruskin University, published in the September 2016 edition of the journal *Personality and Individual Differences*.

Page 73
Social media usage statistics based on the special report *Digital 2025* by the organization We Are Social.

Books we'd like to credit

» Foolproof: Why We Fall for Misinformation and How to Build Immunity **Sander van der Linden**

» The Tiger That Isn't: Seeing Through a World of Numbers **Andrew Dilnot & Michael Blastland**

» Can You Believe It? How to Spot Fake News and Find the Facts **Joyce Grant**

» Bad Science **Ben Goldacre**

» How to Lie with Statistics **Darrell Huff**

» Made You Look: How Advertising Works and Why You Should Know **Shari Graydon**

» Breaking News: How to Tell What's Real From What's Rubbish **Nick Sheridan**

» The Curious Person's Guide to Fighting Fake News **David G. McAfee**

» May Contain Lies: How Stories, Statistics and Studies Exploit Our Biases – And What We Can Do About It **Alex Edmans**

» Misbelief: What Makes Rational People Believe Irrational Things **Dan Ariely**

Additional editing by
Alice Beecham

Additional design by
Maddison Warnes & Kirsty Tizzard

Additional illustration by
Richard Merritt & Kate Sutton

First published in 2026 by
Usborne Publishing Limited, 83-85 Saffron Hill,
London EC1N 8RT, United Kingdom.

usborne.com

Copyright © 2026 Usborne Publishing Limited.

The name Usborne and the Balloon logo are registered trade marks of Usborne Publishing Limited. All rights reserved. No part of this publication may be reproduced or used in any manner for the purpose of training artificial intelligence technologies or systems (including for text or data mining), stored in retrieval systems or transmitted in any form or by any means without prior permission of the publisher.

Please note that the people, usernames, products, and businesses referred to in this book are fictional and not to be construed as real. Any resemblance to actual products, businesses, or persons, living or dead, is entirely coincidental.

Printed in the UK. UKE.